Electric sightseeing buses were popular in the United States in the early years of the twentieth century. This Columbia was built for the Blanke Tea & Coffee Company for use at the St Louis World's Fair of 1904. It seated forty-eight passengers, who entered at the rear via a set of adjustable steps which could be folded into the body when the vehicle was in use. The seats had hinged centre sections so that an aisle could be opened up for the whole length of the car.

ELECTRIC VEHICLES

Nick Georgano

Shire Publications Ltd

CONTENTS

Published in 1996 by Shire Publications Ltd, Cromwell House, Church Street, Princes Risborough, Buckinghamshire HP27 9AA, UK.

Printed in Great Britain by CIT Printing Services, Press Buildings, Merlins Bridge, Haverfordwest, Dyfed SA61 1XF.

British Library Cataloguing in Publication Data: Georgano, G. N. (George Nicolas) Electric Vehicles. – (Shire Album; 325) 1. Electric vehicles – History I. Title 629.2'293'09 ISBN 0-7478-0316-1.

Editorial Consultant: Michael E. Ware, Curator of the National Motor Museum, Beaulieu.

ACKNOWLEDGEMENTS
The author would like to thank the following for their help with information and illustrations: Nick Baldwin, John Chubb, John Dance, Patrick R. Foster, Paul Gray, Keith Marvin, Geoffrey Morant, Richard Pryor, Dr Alan Sutton and Taylor Vinson. Photographs, including the cover, are reproduced by kind permission of the National Motor Museum, Beaulieu, with the exception of the following: pages 26 (lower right), 27 (top) and 30 (lower left), which are by the author; pages 3, 13, 18, 19 (centre left) and 22, from the Nick Baldwin Collection; pages 19 (top left and right) and 25 (right), from the Arthur Ingram Collection; page 17, from the Elliot Kahn Collection; page 30 (lower right), by Richard Pryor; page 26 (centre left), by A. Rushby; and page 5, from the Alan Sutton Collection.

Cover: *1901 Columbia stanhope, 1947 Brush Pony milk float.*

One of the most striking of current electric cars is the Impact, made by General Motors and launched in 1990. Its lead/acid batteries are mounted between the driver and the passenger, and also behind the seats. They give a range of 70-80 miles (110-130 km), though this is drastically reduced if one puts the Impact's acceleration to the test. It can reach 60 mph (97 km/h) in 8.5 seconds, comparable with a BMW 525i. In 1995 the Impact was still a long way from production, even though GM quoted a provisional price of $25,000. A development, the EV1, was planned for production in the summer of 1996.

An early British-built car was the Bushbury Electric Cart, designed by Thomas Parker and with running gear by the Star Cycle Company, later makers of Star cars. The front wheel was steered by reins, and it was highly commended in trials organised by 'The Engineer' at the Crystal Palace in May 1897.

INTRODUCTION

Electric power had a long period of development before it was successfully applied to road vehicles. Put simply, two distinct items are needed: a battery to produce electric current, and a motor to convert this to motive power capable of driving wheels. The principle of the battery rests on the discovery that two elements can interact to produce an electric current. This was discovered by the Italian scientist Luigi Galvani, who in 1786 connected an iron rail to a copper hook by a severed frog's leg and noticed a twitch in the leg: electricity running through the leg caused the muscles to contract. Twelve years later another Italian, Alessandro Volta, constructed what he called a Voltaic pile, silver and zinc discs separated by cardboard soaked in salt water. This could be considered the first battery, as it contained the essential ingredients of all batteries, two dissimilar substances (electrodes) placed in a liquid (electrolyte). The same principle applies in the dry battery, in which the electrolyte is a paste. This was not invented until 1868, by Georges Leclanché. The battery most widely used for electric vehicles is the lead/acid, invented by Gaston Planté in 1859, using different types of lead plate in an electrolyte of dilute sulphuric acid. The great advantage of this over previous batteries is that it can be recharged by applying a current to it. As the battery discharges power, the proportion of water to acid rises until it is mostly water and the plates can no longer yield useful chemical activity. This situation can be

3

reversed by applying a current until the proportion of acid to water is at its maximum again.

A pair of electrodes in an electrolyte is a cell, and a combination of cells makes up a battery. Each fully charged lead/acid cell produces about 2 volts; thus a 6 volt battery has three cells and a 12 volt battery has six. These are the standard sizes used for starting and other purposes in a petrol car. An electric car requires more cells, and a heavy truck up to sixty.

Despite the predominance of the lead/acid battery, many other types have been proposed. An early alternative was the nickel-iron/alkali battery developed by Thomas Edison and known as the Edison cell. This was widespread in electric cars and trucks before 1914. A famous textbook, Rankin Kennedy's *The Book of the Motor Car*, published in 1913, dismissed the lead/acid battery as out of date. 'It will, therefore, not be necessary to consider the lead plate accumulator.' However, the Edison system produces only 1.2 volts per cell.

At least twenty other systems have been proposed, and among the more practical are nickel/zinc, zinc/air, zinc/chlorine hydrate, nickel/hydride and sodium/sulphur. The last is used in the Ford Ecostar and employs liquid 'plates' (sulphur) and a solid electrolyte of sodium set in a long ceramic test-tube placed upright in the can. At a temperature of 600°C both chemicals are liquid, and the sodium can pass through the ceramic wall. This temperature can be maintained by the equivalent of two 100 watt light bulbs. Unfortunately it is not unknown for sodium/sulphur batteries to catch fire. The nickel/hydride gives 50 per cent more storage capacity than the lead/acid, so making it more compact. The battery used in an electric version of the Toyota RAV-4 gives 288 volts, which would require a lead/acid battery of 144 cells.

A lightweight solid lithium battery, already used for camcorders, laptop computers and mobile phones, has attracted the attention of American manufacturers such as Ford and General Motors. Another promising system which differs from others is the EFL (Electric Fuel Limited) in which a zinc electrode is removed and replaced by a fresh one. This takes as little as 100 seconds, and the electrode can be refreshed in special plant.

The basic principle of the electric motor was discovered by Michael Faraday in the 1820s. He demonstrated that if a looped wire containing a current was placed between the poles of a magnet, the wire would rotate because it has become a miniature magnet, and the 'poles' of the wire will be repelled by the poles of the magnet. In order to keep the wire rotating, a commutator is used. This is a metal ring in two halves, to which current from the battery is applied through carbon brushes; the power is constantly switched from one half to the other, ensuring continuous rotation. In Faraday's original experiments a single loop of wire was used, but later motors have many wires wound round a soft iron armature, supported by bearings.

4

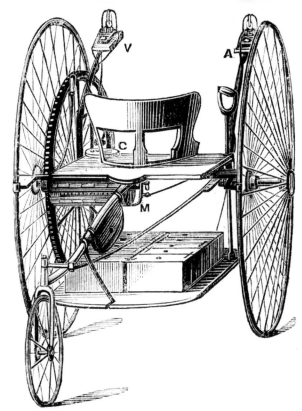

Rear view of Ayrton and Perry's tricycle of 1882. It had a top speed of 8 mph (13 km/h) and, like most self-propelled vehicles at that time, was tested mainly at night. For this reason it had electric lighting, though this was more to aid the reading of the ammeter and voltmeter (A and V in the illustration) than to see the way.

THE PIONEERS

The first electric motor, used to drive a lathe, was patented in 1837 by Thomas Davenport, a blacksmith from Bradon, Vermont, USA. He formed a company to manufacture motors and published the first newspaper exclusively devoted to electrical matters, which he called *The Electromagnet and Mechanic's Intelligencer*. The first vehicles to be powered by batteries and electric motors were both railway locomotives, made by Moses Farmer of Massachusetts in 1847 and Charles Page of Washington, DC, in 1849. More than thirty years passed before anyone tried to make a battery-powered road vehicle, though in Germany Werner von Siemens built and tested a four-seater trolley car, the ancestor of the trolleybus, in 1882.

The reason for the lack of enthusiasm for battery-powered vehicles was the same one that has dogged would-be manufacturers up to the present – the weight of the batteries. In the nineteenth century the problem was considerably worse than it is today; the Grove cells used by Farmer and Page contained lead plates 1 foot (0.3 metre) square and were too heavy for one man to lift. By the 1880s more compact batteries were available, and a few electric vehicles began to appear on both sides of the Atlantic. The honour of making the first went to the French inventor Gustave Trouve, who displayed not only an electrically powered tricycle, but also a boat and a model dirigible, at the International Exhibition of Electricity in Paris in 1881. The tricycle was English-made and the total weight, including six Planté batteries, was 350 pounds (159 kg). Power output was no more than 0.1 horsepower. The first electric vehicle in England was by the distinguished electrical engineers Professors William Edward Ayrton and John Perry. In 1882 they built a tricycle, or possibly adapted an existing pedal tricycle, powered by a 0.5 horsepower mo-

This picture is captioned 'The First Motor Car built and tested in Coventry, in 1888, by the late J. K. Starley, of Starley & Sutton, the founders of the Rover firm.' Unlike the Ayrton tricycle, which was an adapted pedal machine, Starley's tricycle of 1888 was purpose-built though clearly using a bicycle-type frame and wheels. The motor is below the wicker basket containing the batteries.

tor and batteries which together weighed 168 pounds (76 kg). Total weight was about 370 pounds (168 kg). Its feeble performance and the hostile attitude of the authorities caused Ayrton to abandon the experiment, and he probably dismantled it.

Six years later John Kemp Starley, who was making Rover bicycles in Coventry, built a tricycle powered by batteries that were concealed in a wicker basket behind the seats. It was badly underpowered, however, and Starley wisely concentrated on bicycles, laying the foundation for the Rover car company. More successful was Magnus Volk of Brighton. He had designed the electric seafront railway which still runs at Brighton today, and in 1887 he built a four-seater dogcart with back-to-back seating and three wheels, powered by a 0.5 horse-power motor made by the Acme & Immisch Electrical Works of London. The walnut-wood body was made by a local coachbuilder, Job Pack. Volk used the car regularly. 'He, his wife and daughter are to be seen taking their airing along the Parade', reported the Journal of the Society of Arts in January 1888. The first Volk car had a top speed of 9 mph (14 km/h) on a smooth level surface, but a loose surface reduced this to 4 mph (6 km/h), and with two passengers it could not climb a gradient of more than one in thirty.

News of Volk's dogcart reached the Sultan of Turkey through the improbable

Three-wheeled electric dogcart made by Acme & Immisch in 1894. This is generally similar in appearance to Magnus Volk's car of 1888.

A Bersey cab of the first type, with battery box removed. The cabs had electric lighting inside as well as outside; some people felt that the interior lights gave too little privacy. The steering wheel on the vertical column needed twenty-two turns to turn the wheels from lock to lock.

medium of the *Leipzig Zeitung*. Sultan Abdul Hamid II, known as Abdul the Red, was so impressed with what he read that he ordered a replica without concern for the cost. 'No need for discussing price. Send dogcart earliest possible', cabled his chamberlain. The Sultan's dogcart was not an exact replica of the prototype, for the motor had double the power, at 1 horsepower, and in place of the single front wheel were two small ones mounted close together. This gave more stability but still enabled centre-pivot steering to be used, the more modern Ackermann type being little known at the time.

The Sultan was sufficiently pleased with his dogcart to order another one, still with an Acme & Immisch motor but now with a body by the well-known London firm of Thrupp & Maberly. One or two more electric vehicles were made by Volk, and by Acme & Immisch on their own, but there was insufficient demand to justify anything one could call production.

America's first electric vehicle was built by William Morrison of Des Moines, Iowa, in 1890. It was a seven-passenger buggy and had a claimed top speed of 20 mph (32 km/h). Henry Morris and Pedro Salom built a series of advanced electric cars in Philadelphia. Unlike the Morrison, these had two motors of 1$\frac{1}{2}$ horsepower each, one driving each front wheel. Steering was by the smaller rear wheels. The principle of motors geared directly to the driving wheels was widely used in heavier American electric vehicles in the next century. At first each Morris and Salom car carried its own name, in the manner of railway locomotives or ships – *Crawford Wagon*, *Fish Wagon*, *Skeleton Bat* etc – but after they had made a dozen or so they ran out of names and later vehicles were simply called 'Electrobats'. Most of them were supplied as cabs for New York and other cities. The claimed range was 20 miles (32 km) a day for a week, without recharge, but this seems improbably high.

By 1897 the Electric Carriage & Wagon Company, as Morris and Salom had named their company, had a substantial fleet of cabs, especially in New York City. They attracted the attention of Isaac Rice, who bought up the company, forming his own Electric Vehicle Company. This in turn merged with Colonel Pope's Columbia Vehicle Company, which in 1900 was the largest vehicle maker in the world, with more than 1500 deliveries, mostly electrics.

In Europe also the cab trade was attracted by the electric vehicle. The London Electrical Cab Company was founded in 1896 to operate cabs designed by the electrical engineer Walter Bersey. Seventy-five of these ran on London streets between 1897 and 1900. They had 3$\frac{1}{2}$ horsepower Lundell-type motors and a range of 30 miles (48 km). Recharging, which was carried out at the firm's station at Lambeth, took twelve hours. The limited range gave drivers a good excuse to refuse long journeys where they were unlikely to find a return fare.

At first the press and public were pleased

7

The six-seater Jeantaud which its maker entered in the 1895 Paris-Bordeaux-Paris race used thirty-eight Fulmen batteries, each weighing 15 kg (33 pounds). Relays of fresh batteries were sent ahead by chartered train, but the car did not get far because of overheated bearings and a damaged axle.

with the novelty of the electric cab ('This electrical Pegasus is very pleasant, quiet and smooth', said *The Daily News*), but problems soon arose. The cabs were not always reliable, they began to vibrate and rattle and the battery box slid about on the floor. Worst of all, the cost of tyre and battery replacement was much greater than anticipated. The company tried to hire the cabs out to their drivers, but again the cost was too great, and the last Bersey cabs were withdrawn in June 1900.

Walter Bersey entered three cars in the Emancipation Run from London to Brighton in November 1896, but neither his cars nor four Britannia electrics completed the course. In 1935 he admitted that one had made the journey from Brixton by train and that he had even applied mud to make it look as if it had covered the 56 miles (90 km) of the Brighton road!

In Paris the leading maker of electric vehicles was Charles Jeantaud, a carriage builder who offered a variety of designs for cab work, including a hansom with the driver perched behind the passengers. He entered a car in the Paris-Bordeaux-Paris race of 1895, but his greatest claim to fame resulted from the choice of one of his cars by the Comte de Chasseloup-Laubat to set up a speed record for cars. In December 1898, on a standard Jeantaud with a wind-cheating body, he reached 39.24 mph (63.15 km/h) over a flying kilometre. The fastest petrol car, though almost 12 cwt (600 kg) lighter, achieved only 35.5 mph (57.13 km/h). This spurred the Belgian racing driver Camille Jenatzy to reply, first with a standard car of his own design, then in a remarkable-looking machine described by the motor-racing historian Gerald Rose as 'a wonderful blue cigar on wheels, the first real racing freak built'. Named *La Jamais Contente* ('Never Satisfied'), it had a torpedo-shaped body, pointed at each end, with two motors, one to each rear wheel. Between December 1898 and April 1899 the Belgian and the Frenchman held the record in turn several times, but final victory went to Jenatzy with 65.75 mph (105.81 km/h). The Comte gave up the struggle, and the record remained with *La Jamais Contente* for three years, after which it was taken by a steam car at 75 mph (120.70 km/h).

'A wonderful blue cigar on wheels' – 'La Jamais Contente' in which Camille Jenatzy achieved a speed of 65.75 mph (105.8 km/h) in April 1899. The body was by Leon Auscher and Fulmen batteries were used.

As well as hansom cabs, the Riker company of Elizabeth, New Jersey, made this luxurious hansom for private use in 1901. It had battery boxes at the front and rear of the body, and a longer wheelbase than the ordinary hansoms. The price was $3200.

THE GOLDEN AGE 1900-20

At the turn of the century there was no consensus about motive power. Steam, internal combustion and electricity seemed equally poised to prevail. In the United States of America the electric outnumbered its rivals, with Columbia alone making 1500 vehicles in 1900, about twice the number of its nearest rival, the Locomobile steamer. The advantages of the electric car were obvious. Petrol cars had a fairly complex starting procedure and were noisy and smelly, while smooth clutch control and gear-changing were skills mastered by relatively few drivers, most starting their cars with jerky, kangaroo motions. This was avoided in steamers, but their owners had to allow forty-five minutes to start up, with eight separate tasks to be performed. Once on the move, the driver had to keep a careful watch on the pressure, otherwise the car would run out of steam on a hill, and a ten-minute wait would ensue before the climb could

be completed. Also the water tank needed to be replenished every 20 miles (32 km/h).

The electric, on the other hand, needed no start-up time, so long as the batteries were fully charged. Driving was very simple, and there was no vibration, smell or deposits of oil on the road. Speed control and braking were usually by a single pedal which worked in the opposite way to the accelerator on a petrol car. When it was fully depressed the brakes came on, and as it was released the speed rose, through four or five speeds.

In the early years a great variety of body styles used electric power. They ranged from simple open two-seaters, very like contemporary steam or petrol cars in appearance, through four-seater surreys, with or without a fringe on top, to heavy town cars, usually with landaulette bodies and the driver seated on a box like his predecessor the coachman, sometimes accompanied by a liveried footman who would jump down to open the door. Sometimes the footman sat behind the passenger compartment or, as in the Jeantaud cab and the Columbia Dauman victoria, the driver sat there too.

The United States led the way in the manufacture of electric cars and commercial vehicles, though Columbia did not remain the world's largest producer after 1900. In July 1899 there was an exhibition at Madison Square Garden in New York devoted entirely to the electric; five makes exhibited thirty vehicles, from light two-seater stanhopes to a heavy delivery wagon. As one would expect, the lighter vehicles had tubular frames, with pressed steel for the heavier, though Fischer and American used the body as an additional frame member. The lighter machines had cycle-type spoked wheels and pneumatic tyres, while the heavier relied on wooden spokes and solid tyres. In this they followed the practice of internal combustion trucks and, as the electrics carried even heavier loads, many had solid rubber tyres until the late 1920s.

Columbias sold well in Europe, being marketed under the name City & Suburban in Britain and l'Electromotion in France. Their popularity in England was boosted when Queen Alexandra took delivery of a two-seater in 1901. Although she probably did not use it on the roads, she enjoyed driving it around the grounds at Sandringham. The car is now in the National Motor Museum at Beaulieu. Two years later her son the Prince of Wales (later King George V) acquired a City & Suburban town brougham with increased battery capacity which gave a top speed of 16 mph (26 km/h). Most cars sold under the City & Suburban name had London-built bodywork.

The best-known British make was the Electromobile, though this was originally an imported French front-wheel-drive Krieger. By 1902 Electromobile were making their own rear-drive designs, at first with a motor in each rear wheel, then from 1903 with a single motor mounted on the rear axle. By 1910 the popularity of the electric car was waning in Britain, and Electromobile were turning to hire

A City & Suburban town brougham similar to the one bought by the Prince of Wales in 1903. The right-hand passenger is the Parisian actress Liane de Pougy.

The Electromobile company was at its peak in 1907 when this landaulette was built. The passengers are the Duchess of Connaught and her daughter, the Crown Princess of Sweden. The footman was necessary on a horse-drawn carriage so that he could jump down and open the door, the coachman remaining at his post. No longer needed on a self-propelled vehicle, the footman was nevertheless retained by some wealthy families.

work rather than manufacture. For an annual payment of £325 a brougham could be hired with all maintenance and battery charging included. A driver could also be provided, his wages being extra. Electromobiles were also used as taxis in London, some surviving up to 1920.

The period of the greatest popularity of the electric car in Europe was from 1900 to 1910, whereas in the United States it lasted around ten years longer and indeed did not reach its peak until 1914. The most likely explanation is that the electric was essentially a town car, and the USA was a much more urban society. In Britain when a businessman reached a certain

degree of success he was likely to move out of town and set himself up as a country gentleman. While some exceptionally rich Americans such as the Rockefellers and Vanderbilts had country estates, the more modestly wealthy would buy or build a substantial house in the fast-growing suburbs of every large city. These would be on paved roads and within a few miles of the shopping centres, ideal territory for the electric car. Most were owned or at any rate operated by women, who appreciated the silence and ease of driving. With her electric brougham the American matron could visit the shops and pay social calls independent of husband or chauffeur, fully protected from the weather. What she could not do was travel more than about 50 miles (80 km) per day or venture beyond the city's paved roads, but normally she did not want to.

Columbia abandoned electric cars after 1907, the year when what was to be America's most popular electric car, the Detroit, first appeared. It was produced by the former carriage maker William C. Anderson and designed by George M. Bacon. Drive from the motor to the rear axle was by chains at first, replaced by shaft drive in 1911. In 1909 Anderson bought the Elwell-Parker Company of Cleveland, which made motors for the Detroit and some of his rivals. He was now able to make almost the whole car

apart from tyres and wheels, and production boomed. From four hundred in 1908 it reached a thousand two years later and peaked at 4669 in 1914. Most Detroits were the typical high two-door closed broughams, nicknamed 'mobile china closets' because of their extensive areas of glass, but the company also offered other styles, including a two-seater roadster with a long bonnet like that of a petrol car.

The average range of the Detroit Electric was 80 miles (120 km), though on a company-sponsored test in 1913 one covered 211.3 miles (340 km) on a single charge. This was doubtless achieved at very low speeds. As a more recent driver of an electric car said, 'too many bursts of acceleration from the traffic lights and you fail to make it home'.

Opposite page: Women are clearly targeted in this Columbus Electric advertisement of 1912. Sold from 1903 to 1915, the Columbus was a popular make with an output of more than a thousand in 1910. This Model 1220 was a typical 'china closet' coupé of the period and was one of two coupés offered in 1912, differing only in wheelbase. It cost $2500.
Below: The front vehicle is one of the twenty Electromobile cabs put on the London streets in 1908. Ten were still in use in 1920. The flags may date this photograph to the coronation of King George V in 1910.

THE COLUMBUS ELECTRIC

A 1917 Detroit Electric coupé showing the batteries under the bonnet. The 40 cells were divided equally between the front and rear of the car. Detroit was one of the leading American cities for registration of electric cars. Chicago was in first place, with 6000 in 1913, and others included Philadelphia, Cleveland and St Louis, though New York lagged behind, with only 500 registered in 1913. However, one New Yorker with a family of daughters bought five electric cars in one order.

The Detroit was the best-known of America's electrics, but there were many others. The historian Beverly Rae Kimes has traced more than three hundred American-made electric cars, including prototypes. Among the better-known were Baker and Rauch & Lang of Cleveland, who merged in 1915; Milburn, whose light and elegant-looking broughams were used by the American Secret Service; Chicago, who supplied a car to Pope Pius X in 1915; Argo, Borland, Ohio and Woods. Milburn solved the problem of lengthy charging times by mounting the batteries on rollers. 'Simply roll out the discharged ones and roll in a freshly charged set.'

The popularity of the electric car declined rapidly between 1914 and 1920. As much as anything, this was due to increased expectations; in 1914 a top speed of 20 mph (32 km/h) and a range of 50-80 miles (80-130 km) were acceptable. Six years later they were not. The freedom from hand cranking, one of the great appeals of the electric to women, was nullified by the widespread use of the electric starter. Suddenly the 'lady image', which had always clung to the electric car, became an 'old lady image'. Younger women went for a Dodge or Chevrolet coupé, which were much cheaper as well as faster. Milburn were out of business by 1923; Rauch & Lang turned largely to taxicabs in the 1920s; only Detroit soldiered on, making dwindling numbers up to 1939. For the last ten years they mostly bought their bodies from Willys and then Dodge, so that they resembled petrol cars, though it seems that a few of the old style were made for traditionalists, doubtless from existing parts. Total production of

Not all American electric cars were closed coupés. This is a two-passenger runabout by the Waverley company of Indianapolis. Dating from 1909, it was called the Model 74 Stanhope and sold for a modest $1500.

Rauch & Lang of Cleveland, Ohio, and Chicopee Falls, Massachusetts, turned to petrol and electric taxis after they gave up electric cars. This is a 1924 cab operated by the Electrotaxi Company of Philadelphia. They did not sell as well as the petrol versions and production ended in 1928.

Detroit Electrics has been estimated at thirty thousand.

Electric cars continued to be used during the 1940s, almost always by old ladies, though they received a brief boost during the wartime years of petrol rationing. In Los Angeles a Red Cross nurse drove a 1917 Detroit Electric regularly from 1943 to 1945. Keith Marvin remembers an old lady with a hat like Queen Mary's riding around the streets of Troy, New York, well into the 1940s.

In Europe the electric car disappeared more quickly. Electromobile had largely turned to hire work by 1910, and in Paris the predominant taxicab makes such as Jeantaud, Jenatzy and Krieger had largely given way to Renault by the same date. Unlike Jeantaud and Jenatzy, Louis-Antoine Krieger (1868-1951) made mostly front-drive vehicles. This came naturally as his first product of 1897 was a two-wheeled attachment for horse-drawn carriages, powered by a motor in each wheel. This gave four-wheel braking as there were separate brakes on the rear wheels. Krieger's first complete electric car came in 1898, and he was soon in business on quite a large scale, selling manufacturing licences to Britain (British Electromobile Company), Germany (Lloyd) and Italy (STAE). After the First World War the electric passenger car was even scarcer in Europe than in the United States, though a few oddities surfaced from time to time. In Germany inflation and poverty led to a crop of cyclecars in the 1920s, and some of these were electrics. In 1935 Partridge, Wilson & Company of Leicester, makers of milk floats, offered a four-seater coupé with petrol-car styling and body by Arthur Mulliner. 64 volt batteries gave a top speed of 27 mph (43 km/h) and a range of 40 miles (64 km), short by comparison with American electrics of an earlier era. It was priced at £385, expensive compared with a Morris Ten at £200. It is not surprising that only forty were sold. Even rarer was the Cleco, a tiny coupé by another milk-float maker. With a wheelbase of only 6 feet 4 inches (193 cm), it had the appearance of a stunted Volkswagen Beetle. A range of 90 miles (145 km) was claimed, but at a speed of only 14 mph (23 km/h), and with a price of £375, or three Morris Eights, only six were sold.

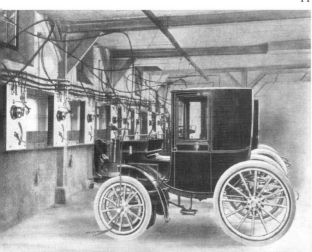

Krieger cabs, c.1900, at their recharging station. Krieger probably made more cabs and commercial vehicles than passenger cars. After 1905 he turned to petrol-electric drive. His name reappeared on a light electric van in 1926, and finally on Milde-Krieger cars in the Second World War

The largest vehicle made by Columbia in 1899 was this twelve-passenger omnibus with stagecoach-type seating above the roof. Top speed was 11 mph (18 km/h). Next to it is Columbia's first petrol-engined car, the Mark VIII Gasoline Runabout.

ELECTRIC COMMERCIAL VEHICLES 1900-39

Electric power was always more suited to commercial work than to the private car. Low speed was less of a disadvantage and batteries could be charged overnight in the operating companies' workshops. There have been two main eras of the electric goods vehicle: heavy trucks of up to 10 tons payload flourished until the late 1920s; and, just as they were disappearing, the light vehicle for milk or bread delivery arrived to take over from the horse.

In the United States Riker and Columbia were the pioneer makes, but the former were discontinued in 1903 as they were similar to Columbias and made in the same factory. Under the Riker name were offered vans, hotel buses and trucks up to 2½ tons payload, but Columbias were larger, reaching 5 tons by 1903. These heavy trucks had two motors powered by Exide batteries of forty-four cells, giving a range of 25 miles (40 km) at 6 mph (10 km/h). Drive was by double reduction gears to the rear axle. The driver sat at least 5 feet (1.5 metres) from the ground, with a vertical steering column. To assist what must have been extremely heavy steering, there was an electric motor activated by the steering wheel.

Columbia was the most popular American electric truck at a time when they outnumbered petrol-engined trucks for heavy work. In 1907, out of eighteen thousand electric trucks at work in the eastern states, eight thousand were Columbias. Other makes included Couple Gear, CT, GV, Quadray, Walker and Ward. Couple Gear,

The 1905 Quadray 6 ton van featured four-wheel drive via a 3½ horse-power motor in each wheel, and four-wheel steering. Note the large steering wheel with vertical column. Some of these heavy electrics had power-assisted steering.

16

FIVE-TON BOSTON CARAVAN

*"Floors" 27 bbls. of sugar. Low platform suitable for Boston
loading-conditions.*

Couple-Gear Front-Drive

WHEN a haulage-problem is extraordinary in its severity, the repu-
tation of "Couple-Gear" comes to mind. In previous years we
have confined our manufacturing operations to four-wheel-drive trucks
and our sales have been mostly for extraordinary work.

We now announce the truck which will do the favorable-to-horse
kind of work at a saving so large that there is no alternative except to provide the necessary funds for so paying an investment. It is the Couple-
Gear Front-Drive— ·

GETS THE LOAD OFF THE RUBBER!

*This 5 ton platform truck was the heaviest of the front-drive Couple Gears which had large
wagon-type rear wheels. These, it was claimed, pulled and rode more easily and cut less into soft
ground. Each front wheel contained its own motor, which acted from each end of the shaft directly
on the inside of the rim. As well as selling complete trucks, Couple Gear sold these motor wheels
separately. 'Your local wagon builder can do the work and save you money', they said.*

Two Edisons and a Walker at a demonstration of goods vehicles in London in 1922. The Edison name was carried by lorries and buses in Britain, but they had General Motors chassis and Edison batteries. In the United States they were sold under the GMC name, but the cachet of the famous electric pioneer Thomas Alva Edison led to the use of his name in Britain.

from Grand Rapids, Michigan, and Quadray, from Detroit, both had four-wheel drive via a motor in each wheel, also offering four-wheel steering on some models. In their catalogue Couple Gear stressed that their front-wheel-drive trucks *'are not designed for speed.* Freight to be hauled economically must be hauled slowly, and the machine which does it must be *adapted* to slow-speed service.'

Slow they were, but consequently very long-lasting. These heavy electric trucks crept around American cities like giant tortoises well into the 1930s, when many were twenty or thirty years old. The record was held by the CT trucks of the Curtis Publishing Company, of *Saturday Evening Post* fame. Built around 1911, they were gradually updated with improvements such as enclosed cabs and were still used for newsprint haulage up to the late 1950s. Electric trucks were used for every kind of haulage, being particularly employed for transport of beer, coal, sand, ice, lumber and refuse. More specialised work included carrying safes and refrigerators, while a steel-carrying Couple Gear was loaded with steel bars extending more than the truck's length at both front and rear. Some Couple Gears were provided with drivers' seats and control at both ends of the chassis.

Manufacture of heavy electric trucks

dwindled during the 1920s as their low speed became more of a drawback. Their long life damaged sales of new models, a problem also encountered with the electric cars and today's milk floats. Lighter electric vans, mainly for door-to-door delivery of milk, bread and laundry, were made in the United States up to the Second World War. The best-known make was Walker, a Chicago firm whose products had motors mounted on the rear axle and an internal gear drive in the rear wheels. Like other electrics, nearly all had forward control, apart from the stylish Model 10 $^3/_4$ ton panel delivery van which sported a long bonnet like a petrol van. Walkers sold well in England, users including the London stores Harrods and Selfridges.

Heavy electric trucks were rarer in England and were not seen until the 1920s. They were made by a diverse range of companies: Clayton, Garrett and Ransomes were well-known builders of steam wagons and traction engines, while the General Vehicle Company was a branch of the American firm of that name, products of both being sold under the name GV. In 1924 this Birmingham firm built one of the largest battery-electric vehicles ever, a 10 ton articulated six-wheeler called the GV Giant. GV also made rigid six-wheelers, of which a number were

A pair of long-lived GV lorries. Dating from 1923, they were still in use by Meux's brewery when photographed at Nine Elms Lane, London, in September 1950.

Clayton of Lincoln were well-known in the steam-wagon and traction-engine field. They made battery-electric trucks in the 1920s, of which the chain-drive $3^{1}/2$ ton refuse collector at work in Leicester is a typical example. It dates from about 1925. With a high-sided vehicle and no rear-loading compaction, refuse collection was harder and slower work in those days.

The GV Giant articulated 10 tonner was the largest British-built battery electric vehicle. Made in 1924 for Manchester Corporation, it had a platform 16 by 7 feet (4.9 by 2.1 metres) and an overall length of 38 feet (11.6 metres). It was used for carrying cable drums of up to 7 tons. The front-opening door is unusual and would be illegal today.

supplied to the City of Birmingham for refuse-collection work. Birmingham was the most faithful user of municipal electrics and ran a large fleet from 1919 to 1971, with the last new vehicle being delivered in 1948. Over the years a total of 262 electric refuse trucks were bought, from nine different manufacturers.

Although much less familiar than the goods vehicle, the battery-electric bus made several appearances, including recent developments which are covered in the final chapter. As early as February 1889 a battery-powered bus built by Radcliffe Ward was tried on the streets of London. It never ran in service, neither did a horse-bus conversion tried in Liverpool in 1894. However, in 1906 the London Electrobus Com-

The only one to have been preserved of seventy-two Electricars DV4 4 ton refuse vehicles bought by the City of Birmingham between 1938 and 1948. Number 184 was in use until 1971 and is now in the Birmingham Museum of Science and Industry.

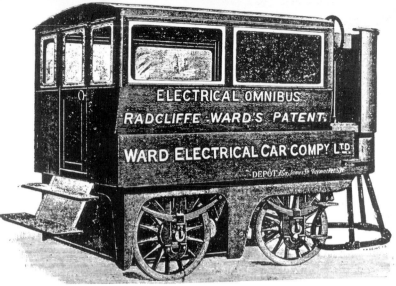

Radcliffe Ward's Electrical Omnibus of 1889. The Financial Times reported a speed of 7 mph (11 km/h) and said that the driver 'can calculate to a nicety the course that he should take'. Nicety or no, Ward's bus never ran in service.

pany was formed to operate a fleet of double-deckers, these having chassis assembled by the Electric Vehicle Company of West Norwood. A number of French components were used, including Thomson Houston motors. The forty-four cell batteries gave a range of 40 miles (64 km). A fleet of twenty Electrobuses ran in London from July 1907 to 1910.

More widespread were the Edison single-deckers which ran in Derby, Lancaster, Loughborough, South Shields, West Bromwich and York at various times between 1914 and 1922. In France De Dion Bouton made a few forty-seater single-deckers in the 1920s, but the last large pre-war battery-electric bus ran in Guernsey in 1936-7. This had a chassis by A. E. Morrison of Leicester and a single-decker body, seating thirty-two, by the Guernsey Railway Company. It was fitted with large balloon tyres, which were said to give it a rolling ride. Combined with perimeter seating, this made it unpopular with passengers and it was withdrawn after fourteen months' service.

In the early 1930s the horse had

been replaced in every form of British road transport except local delivery work, notably by the dairies and railway companies, both of which owned thousands of horses. That the horse was eventually ousted from dairy work as well was largely due to the light electric vehicle, one of the most important developments in battery-vehicle history. It came at an opportune time, when heavier machines, for loads of 3 tons and above, were fast losing popularity. Credit for the lighter type is due initially to two companies, GV and A. E. Morrison & Sons

Britain's second battery bus was operated by the Electric Motive Power Company in Liverpool in 1894. It consisted of a garden-seat horse-bus fitted with batteries and a motor.

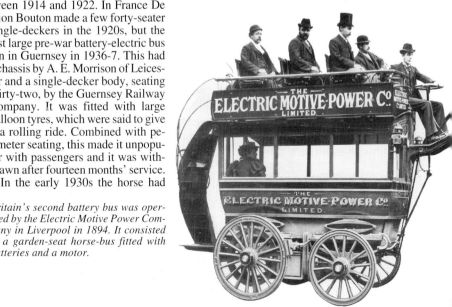

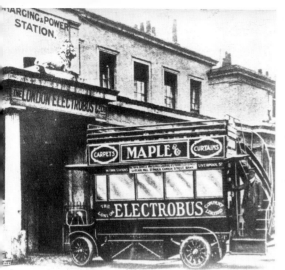

The only battery buses that ran with any success in London were those of the London Electrobus Company Ltd. Introduced in July 1907, a fleet of twenty ran for three years. This one is operating the Victoria to Liverpool Street route. In 1910 they were sold to the Brighton, Hove & Preston United Omnibus Company, who had bought three of their own the previous year. They dismantled four of the ex-London buses for spares. The last Electrobus ran in Brighton in 1917.

Ltd of Leicester, who had been in business making bicycles, trade tricycles and electrical equipment. In 1933 they combined their expertise in a light delivery vehicle for a 10 cwt (508 kg) load. A 48 volt 15 amp/hour battery gave a range of about 50 miles (32 km), and the chassis was of pressed steel with wire wheels of distinctly cycle-type appearance, though later Morrisons used pressed steel wheels. Like almost all subsequent vehicles of this type, the body had forward control.

Morrison was soon joined by other manufacturers, of which Midland, Victor and Wilson were the best-known. They all followed the same general design, using proprietary components such as Bendix brakes, Hardy Spicer prop shafts and Exide, DP or Young batteries. Payloads extended downwards as well as upwards. Morrison offered a 5 cwt (254 kg) van in 1935, and even smaller were the pedestrian-controlled three-wheelers made by T. H. Lewis, with a 3 1/2 cwt (178 kg) payload and selling for only £89 10s. Logically, most electric vans had forward control to maximise load area, but some makers thought a bonnet made them more stylish. The light electric's success was rapid, with new registrations in Great Britain rising by 50 per cent between 1934 and 1935. By 1938 there were 4340 electrics registered (compared with 1303 in 1933), and in 1946 the figure had risen to 7828.

In Europe the larger electric truck was still in the ascendant. France's leading make was Sovel, founded in 1925. They were made in sizes up to five-tonners and featured two motors, one driving each rear wheel by chain, thus doing away with the

One of the De Dion Bouton forty-seaters put into service in Lyons in 1924. Some of these were still in use in 1938, along with more modern battery buses by Renault and Vetra. By then they had covered about 300,000 km (186,420 miles) each and were said to be good for many more years service. The forty cells were carried in a wooden crate between the axles.

Above left: *A pioneer of the new type of small electric van suitable for local delivery work was the GV, introduced in 1933 and made in two sizes, 5/7 cwt and 10/15 cwt. This is a 5/7 cwt model, which had a wheelbase of only 5 feet (1.5 metres). A bonneted version had the same load capacity but a 6 foot 6 inch (2.0 metre) wheelbase. Bakeries and dairies were the main customers for the light electric.*

Above right: *Familiar sights in London for more than thirty years were the Harrods vans. Designed by J. H. L. Bridge of Harrods Garage and built in the company's workshops at Barnes in south-west London, they used electrical equipment by Bruce Peebles & Company, and some components were carried over from the Walkers which Harrods used for many years. Wheels were 1933 Morris Commercial type. They had a range of 60 miles (100 km). Sixty were built between 1936 and 1939, and the last was not withdrawn until 1970. One went to the Science Museum, one to the National Motor Museum, and two were retained by Harrods.*

need for a differential. French-built American Ironclad batteries were used, and the Jacquet motors were mounted at first ahead of the rear axle, then behind it driving forward. This gave an unusual appearance, as the normal chain drive in any vehicle, petrol or electric, ran from a countershaft back to the axle.

In Germany the electric was widely used between the wars, with at least a dozen manufacturers making vehicles from 1/2 ton up to 10 tons payload, the latter being rigid six-wheelers by Esslingen. They were widely used for postal work; in 1926 Berlin alone had six hundred Bergmann bonneted 2 1/2 ton vans, some of which were still in service in East Berlin in the 1960s. In 1937 the German postal authorities operated 2400 electric vehicles. Esslingen offered an electric fire engine in 1941, and refuse collectors were made in considerable quantities by Bergmann, Bleichert, Elite, Faun and others. A peculiarly German type was the electric road tractor; typical was the Bleichert ES400 with two 8.8 kW motors, capable of pulling trailers up to 10 tons. Even more powerful was the Elite-Muchow of 1936, a forward-control tractor with motors totalling 30 kW, a top speed of 19 mph (30 km/h), a range of 78 miles (125 km) and a drawbar pull of 15 tons.

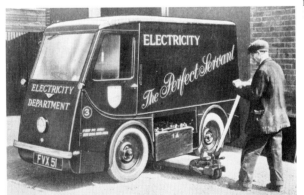

A Metrovick 7/9 cwt van of 1938, showing the quick change of batteries on a trolley. These vans were made by a branch of the large Metropolitan-Vickers Electrical Company. In production from 1934 to 1942, they had box-section chassis and either worm or spiral bevel final drive.

Peugeot's VLV (Voiture Legère de Ville), of which 377 were made during the Second World War. Four 12 volt batteries under the bonnet ensured a range of 50 miles (80 km). At 20 mph (32 km/h) the Safi motor turned at 2250 rpm. Overall length was 8 feet 9 inches (2.67 metres).

ELECTRIC VEHICLES IN THE SECOND WORLD WAR

Practically every country suffered from fuel shortage to a greater or lesser degree during the Second World War, but this did not lead to a proliferation of electric vehicles, with the exception of occupied France. There a combination of native ingenuity and an almost complete withdrawal of petrol supplies brought about many clever solutions. Jacques Borgé and Nicolas Viasnoff, in their book *Les Vehicules de l'Occupation*, claim that more than fifty different types of light electric were made, the majority being unique home-built vehicles. In the absence of steel, construction utilised wood, plywood and aluminium. Some were pro-

duced commercially, both passenger and goods vehicles, the biggest constructor being Peugeot, who made 377 of their VLV cabriolet between June 1941 and February 1945. Unlike some of its rivals, it was not an adaptation of an existing design, having a light two-seater body, with the rear wheels set close together, independent front suspension by transverse leaves and rear suspension by a single longitudinal spring. Other firms which built electrics from scratch included four famous names, Delaunay-Belleville, Georges Irat, Hispano-Suiza and Mors, as well as the aircraft maker Breguet, Pierre Faure, Louis Renard and

The CGE-Tudor was the best-looking of the French wartime electrics. Designed by Jean Grégoire, it had a cast aluminium frame which Grégoire had used in the pre-war Amilcar Compound, with which it shared a number of components. Normal range was 56 miles (90 km), but in September 1942 Grégoire covered 158 miles (254 km) between Paris and Tours on a single charge. A coupé was shown at the first post-war Paris Salon in October 1946, but no production followed.

CGE-Tudor, whose car was designed by Jean Grégoire. The last was of advanced aluminium construction and had a normal range of 56 miles (90 km) per charge. Production of the Grégoire was authorised by the Germans on condition that the majority were exported to Germany. Though two cars a week were made for nearly two years, so far as is known none left France. One was offered to the director of a biscuit factory in exchange for his weight in biscuits, and everyone was happy with the transaction!

The other route for makers of electric vehicles was to use existing chassis and bodies, either replacing the petrol engines with batteries and electric motors, or acquiring the frames and installing electric power from scratch. The best-known example of the latter was the Milde-Krieger, whose names dated back to the nineteenth century. They turned out a number of saloons based on the 6/7CV La Licorne. In the commercial field, they converted the forward-control Chenard-Walcker van, as did Fenwick the Citroën TUB and TUC. About a hundred Fenwick

Urbels were made, some used as ambulances. When Citroën discontinued the TUC early in 1942, Fenwick turned to a new van, the Hippelec, which was simply a railway platform truck with body and cab. Meanwhile the traditional electric trucks of Sovel continued to be made, and another Lyons firm, Stela, made a five-passenger electric taxi. Admiral Darlan, head of the Vichy government, had two for his personal use.

Most building of electric vehicles in France came to an end in July 1942, when their manufacture and conversion were forbidden throughout occupied France. Peugeot seem to have carried on with the VLV, and Sovels and Stelas were continued as Lyons was outside the occupied area.

Elsewhere in Europe, Holland made a few light cars similar to the French models, while in Spain, neutral and at peace after their civil war, David made some electric cars and taxis, and Autarquia built 3 ton trucks, vans and buses on the Ford Model 51 chassis.

24

Below: *Wales & Edwards was another maker new to the market after the war. They were best-known for their three-wheelers, made from 1950 to date, though they also made four-wheelers from 1968. This is an unusual five-wheeled articulated milk float made in 1961. Known as the Loadmaster 2 tonner, it had an overall length of 19 feet (5.8 metres). Only eighteen were made. Since 1992 W & E Electric Vehicles has been owned by Smith's Electric Vehicles.*

Above: *Among the new makes of electric vehicle after the Second World War was Brush. The Loughborough-based firm was a well-known bodybuilder to the bus industry and also a maker of electrical equipment. Their vehicles were three- and four-wheelers, the former being known as the Pony. This Utility built in 1947 on the 25-30 cwt (1270-1524 kg) chassis had a Brush-built body to carry eleven adults or twenty small children. It was converted to a public address van in 1949.*

DECLINE AND REVIVAL

For the first twenty years after the Second World War there was little interest in electric vehicles as passenger cars. There was no anxiety about fossil-fuel supplies, nor was pollution an issue. In Britain the electric milk float was still widely used, and numbers reached their peak in the 1970s, with more than fifty thousand registered. New makes which catered for this market included NCB (Northern Coachbuilders) and Wales & Edwards, whose three-wheelers are still very familiar. On the continent heavier vehicles prevailed, with Sovel making trucks up to 5 tons capacity, and German makes such as Esslingen, Gaubschat and Lloyd offered trucks and vans of similar size, especially for postal work, but only up to the mid 1950s. Small electrics, at first mostly made in Britain, were widely used in Swiss mountain resorts such as Wengen and Zermatt, where petrol vehicles were not allowed.

In the United States several small firms offered light two-passenger 'shopping cars', mostly made in California and related to the golf cart (which had been pioneered in the USA in 1930). More ambitious was the Henney Kilowatt, an electric conversion of the Renault Dauphine, offered by a former hearse maker of Bloomington, Illinois, from 1960 to 1964. It had twelve 6 volt batteries and a range of 40 miles (64 km). Production is uncertain; one hundred Dauphine bodies were ordered, but possibly not all were sold. Renault seemed to be a popular base, for two years after the Henney Kilowatt vanished there appeared the Mars 11 with Renault 10 body. This had four 30 volt battery packs of five lead-cobalt batteries each, with a claimed 77 horsepower available for peak acceleration and a range of 70-120 miles (110-190 km). Despite these advantages over the Henney, the Mars lasted only year, and probably very few were made. It is said that it was the first electric car to circle the Indianapolis track.

By the late 1960s, several years before the energy crisis struck, the big American corporations began to show interest in the electric car. Ford tested a Mark II Cortina with lead-acid batteries, and General Motors ran an Opel Kadett which used lead-acid for acceleration

Ross Auto electric vehicles were made in Southport from 1950 until the late 1980s. Despite its tiny wheels and 6 foot 6 inch (2.0 metre) wheelbase, this model 25 of 1960 was rated at 25 cwt (1270 kg) payload.

and zinc-air batteries for range. This was a *tour de force* when cost was no object but would hardly have been a commercial proposition. Another dual-battery car was the 1968 Delta by General Electric which used lead/acid for acceleration, orion/nickel for cruising. In 1978 General Electric brought out the Centennial, a two-door sedan with eighteen 6 volt lead/acid batteries which could be recharged in six hours. A standard 12 volt battery linked to the on-board charger powered the radio, windscreen wipers, defroster, fans and headlights. This was a sophisticated concept but, like all the others from large corporations, it was an experimental and promotional vehicle only.

Below: Electric vehicles flourish in Swiss mountain resorts where internal combustion is banned. This Pfander took passengers and their luggage from the station at Wengen to their hotel. In Switzerland's other car-free resort, Zermatt, only hotels with more than thirty-one beds were allowed to have their own bus, and its dimensions were restricted to 4 by 1.4 metres (13 feet 2 inches by 4 feet 7 inches). Pfander was one of the leading Swiss manufacturers of electric vehicles, making platform trucks and tractors, tipper trucks and specialised machines for cleaning airliners at Zürich and Geneva airports.

Above: The longevity of the running gear of electric vehicles has led to much rebuilding, particularly by the Midlands Co-operative Society. This van went into service in 1962 as a Morrison-Electricar laundry van with composite cab and body. It was later rebuilt as a milk float, retaining the original cab and parts of the body, then re-cabbed in fibreglass and rebodied by the Midlands Co-op, still as a milk float, and finally, in the 1990s, fitted with a new van body for the Belfry Hotel and Golf Lounge.

Left: Typical of the larger continental electrical vehicles, this is a 4 ton van for the Austrian Post Office, made in the 1950s by OAF, a company descended from the Austrian branch of Fiat.

The most prolific American electric car of recent years was the Sebring-Vanguard, made in this form from 1974 to 1976, and as the Comuta-Car with heavier bumpers from 1979 to 1985. Small batches of ten were made in 1986 and 1987, and a three-wheeler called the Triton was made in limited numbers in 1989-90. Total production of all cars and vans was about four thousand. The Vanguard had a tubular frame and disc front brakes.

It was left to much smaller concerns to attempt commercial production. The most successful in the United States were the Sebring-Vanguard (1972-6) and its successor the Comuta-Car (1977-85). Early models were described unkindly as 'looking a little bit like a cross between a golf cart and a telephone booth', but from 1974 a better-looking car was built, though still with angular lines. The two-passenger coupé was powered by eight 6 volt batteries driving through a General Electric direct-current motor. There was also a van version, 150 of which were bought by the US Postal Service, and others were bought by the Long Island Lighting Company and the Salt River Project of Phoenix, Arizona. Production of the Sebring-Vanguard reached 2153, and a further 1800 (approximately) were made under the Comuta-Car and Comuta-Van names. Among users of the Comuta-Van was Gamma Photo Labs of Chicago, which operated two. Their owner, Jerome August, found that energy costs were low, about 1 cent per mile compared with 5-6 cents for a petrol van, but cold weather presented problems, with reduced range and poor traction on slippery streets.

Other users operated battery vans with mixed success. In 1970 the Edison Electric Institute bought 107 Battronic vans with Boyertown bodies, for various members of the Institute. They had a range of 68 miles (109 km) at 20 mph (32 km/h), 42 miles (68 km) at 30 mph (48 km/h) and only 30 miles (48 km) at 40 mph (64 km/h), a clear demonstration of the inverse ratio of range to speed which bedevils all battery vehicles. Problems were

Announced in 1976, the Transformer 1 was an advanced and luxurious car made by Electric Fuel Propulsion of Detroit; it featured a leather interior, air conditioning and stereo tape deck. The battery was a lead/cobalt system, said to give more than twice the energy per pound compared with lead/acid, and to be rechargeable in forty-five minutes. Top speed was 70 mph (113 km/h). All this did not come cheap, and a price of $30,000 was quoted, though few, if any, were sold to the public. A Cadillac-based six-seater followed in 1979 and two years later came the Silver Volt conversion of a Buick Century station wagon. Full production was promised for 1982, but nothing materialised.

Left and below: *Ford of Britain announced the Comuta in 1967. A typical two-passenger town coupé, it was compact enough for three parked end-on to the kerb to take up no more space than a single normal car. The batteries occupied the central part of the backbone chassis, while transverse ribs at the front held the steering column, pedals and shock absorbers, and at the rear the reduction gear case which carried the two motors. Like all the battery cars built by large firms, the Comuta did not go into production.*

encountered with control circuits, the brake-acceleration system and weak axles. A number of vans quickly became immobilised and were parked in a corner to be forgotten. Three Battronic buses were supplied to Lansing, Michigan, with the same results. In 1971 325 Jeep-based AM General electric vans were ordered by the US Post Office, which operated a large number of similar petrol-engined vans. They found that time out of use was 55 per cent less than for internal combustion vans, while fuel consumption, based on thermal units of fuel delivered to electricity companies, was 75-90 per cent of that delivered to the refineries for petrol production. On the other hand, the initial costs were higher, especially for batteries, and there was the usual drawback of limited range. No further orders were placed for the electric vans.

During the 1970s worldwide interest in battery vehicles increased dramatically. By the end of the decade cars or small commercial vehicles had been built in Australia, Belgium, Brazil, Bulgaria, Canada, Denmark, France, Germany, Great Britain, Holland, Hong Kong, India, Italy, Japan, Mexico, the Soviet Union, Sweden, Switzerland and Taiwan. Other countries which have entered the field since 1980 have included the Czech Republic, Finland, Korea, Poland and Spain. Many have been conversions of existing petrol vehicles, and few have won many commercial sales. Notable ventures in Britain have included the Enfield, backed by the Greek shipowner John Goulandris and built in his yards on the island of Syros, and the Lucas

taxi and conversions of Bedfords.

The Enfield 9000 was a two-passenger saloon with steel-tube frame, all-coil suspension, aluminium body and 8 horsepower

The Enfield runabout was rarer than the saloon. Sometimes called the Bikini, it was made in hardtop form, as here, or with a canvas top and no doors. Like the saloons, it had eight lead/acid six-cell batteries which weighed 85 pounds (38.5 kg) each.

motor. Speed was claimed to be 'up to 40 mph (64 km/h)' and range 'up to 44 miles (71 km) on flat and level roads'. A total of 108 Enfields were made between 1969 and 1976, including a few open runabouts. Sixty-one were bought by the Electricity Council.

Lucas Industries began their programme of electric-vehicle research in 1968 with a converted Bedford CA. Initially the batteries were located in the van's load space, but later they were accommodated in a detachable pannier beneath the floor, so the van had the same capacity as the petrol version. Most of the Lucas vehicles were based on the Bedford CF; twenty were made in the 1970s and tested by a wide variety of operators, including the Royal Mail, Post Office Telecoms and the Midlands Electricity Board. A 216 volt lightweight traction battery and a 40 kW motor provided motive power, while a standard 12 volt battery powered basic equipment such as lights. Range was 70 miles (113 km) and top speed 50 mph (80 km/h), though not at the same time. As well as the vans, Lucas made a limousine version, of which two were supplied to the Duke of Edinburgh, who still uses one occasionally. In addition to the Bedfords, Lucas made two examples of a purpose-designed taxi which were tested on the streets of London.

More recently an electric conversion of the Ford Escort van, named Ecostar, has been tested with a number of users including Hampshire Police. Sodium/sulphur batteries provide 330 volts to power a motor rated at 75 horsepower. The batteries are three times as powerful as lead/acid ones and give a range of 100 miles (160 km), with speeds up to 70 mph (113 km/h). At its maximum the motor turns at 13,500 rpm. Useful features of the Ecostar are a gauge showing the number of miles left before a recharge is needed, and solar cells to power the ventilation fan. Ecostar, of which Ford planned a run of 105 in 1995, is one of the most sophisticated electric vehicles there is, yet the makers admit that the sodium/sulphur batteries would be prohibitively expensive to make in quantity. Nevertheless Ford plan to use the Ecostar's system in a Fiesta-sized car by 2000.

One of the most radical uses of the electric car is the communal car concept, where subscribers to the scheme pick up a car from a park and leave it at another when the journey is completed – a sort of self-drive taxi. The idea was pioneered in Amsterdam in 1974, with tiny three-wheelers called Witkars, and has been revived in France in 1995. PSA, the consortium making Citroën and Peugeot cars, placed a fleet

of electric-powered Citroën AXs and Peugeot 106s, twenty-five of each, in La Rochelle. They proved generally popular, though customers complained of limited range and the nuisance of finding plug-in recharging points. The idea is taken a step further in the TULIP (Transport Urbain Libre Individual et Public) system also backed by PSA and planned for 1996. This uses a purpose-built tiny two-seater bubble-shaped coupé only 7 feet (2.1 metres) long, powered by nickel/cadmium batteries and a 9.6 kW motor driving the front wheels. There will be a subscription, with an hourly charge for use of the car. There is no need to plug in for charging, as this is done by parking over a charger, which acts by induction. Reservations and billing are controlled by the subscriber's 'magic key', which also unlocks and activates the car. The key also contains a mobile phone pad. TULIP will be tried out in Tours in 1996.

The Witkar scheme failed through being too modestly capitalised. It is to be hoped that TULIP, backed by France's largest car maker, public transport operator Via-GTI and toll systems expert Cegelic, will fare better. In the late 1980s and early 1990s several major manufacturers have offered electric conversions of their small cars. These include the Citroën AX, Peugeot 106 and 205, and Fiat Panda and 500. However, the numbers sold have been very small. A joint venture between Mercedes-Benz and the Swiss watch company Swatch plans to produce a very small city car by 1998. This will be offered in electric form, with hub motors in each wheel, as well as

BMW's contribution to electric-car development was the E2, an attractive two-door saloon aimed at the California market, where pollution regulations are at their strictest and there is a highly optimistic plan to ban all internal combustion engines from large cities by 2007.

with petrol and diesel engines.

Many small firms have offered vehicles since 1985, and some are still available. These include electric versions of the French microcars, by Erad, Ligier and Microcar. Switzerland has produced at least ten designs, including one which can be

The diminutive Swiss-built Horlacher coupé, being charged from solar panels on the roof of the Hotel du Lac in Interlaken. Solar panels have also been used on the cars themselves, and endurance tests have been held in the United States and Australia.

Britain's first electric kit car, the AVT-100E, seats four, with luggage, and has a top speed of 75 mph (120 km/h). It can be bought in various stages of assembly, from complete kit at £2500 to ready for the road at £12,000. AVT, of Hatch Beauchamp, Somerset, also supply conversion kits for the Metro.

charged from solar panels on the roof of a house or hotel. Nevertheless, the number of electric cars registered in Switzerland remains very low, sixty in 1993 and sixty-five in 1994. In Germany an attractive small coupé, the Hotzenblitz, was due to be made at the rate of two per day in the former Simson motorcycle works. In Britain a Kent importer offered four vehicles for 1995, the French-built Microcar Lyra two-seater, and three vans: the Elcat, which is a Finnish conversion of the Subaru E12, the French Volta 500 kg van and the Swedish Tugger three-wheeler single-seater with 300 kg payload.

There have been a large number of prototypes and trials of commercial vehicles but, apart from the familiar fields of milk floats, airport and hospital vehicles and fork-lift trucks, there has been little large-scale use of electrics. In France the long-lived Sovel company closed in 1977, though a later large electric refuse truck with a 7$\frac{1}{2}$ ton payload was the SITA, which used a Renault cab and chassis and four motors, one of 40 horsepower for propulsion, and smaller ones for the compaction system, power steering and brakes. This added considerably to the cost, and though its silence commended it for municipal work, the SITA did not survive the 1980s. In England the milk float remains the most familiar electric vehicle, though numbers are dwindling. Its longevity tells against it, for operators often keep their vehicles for twenty years or more, rebuilding where necessary. Also the decline in doorstep milk delivery is a serious threat to the industry. In 1950 seventeen firms in Britain made specialised battery road vehicles. In 1995 there were only two, Smith's Electrics of Gateshead, who also make the W & E three-wheelers, and

Bradshaw of Peterborough, making modified versions of the American Taylor-Dunn.

In 1974 two Seddon buses converted to battery power ran in Manchester, while battery buses based on the nineteen-seater Dodge 50 were used in the 1980s in Bournemouth and by the South of Scotland Electricity Board. In 1994 the Iveco hybrid buses operated in Torquay. Each carries an on-board charger powered by a 997 cc Fiat petrol engine, avoiding the need for lengthy overnight charging. By the end of 1994 they had been transferred to Exeter. In Oxford six similar Ivecos worked a 'Park and Glide' service. Four all-electric Metroriders also ran in Oxford.

On the continent full-size battery buses have been built by MAN and Mercedes-Benz and have been tested in a number of German cities. Battery vans and buses still reign supreme in some Swiss mountain resorts, and those in Zermatt are larger than most, seating up to seventeen. Battery buses of midibus size or above are currently in use in Baltimore, Denver, Los Angeles, New York, Lowell (Massachusetts), and other American cities, also in Rome and in Srinagar, India.

At the end of 1995 the battery vehicle seems set to become a significant mode of transport in several countries. Environmental pressures favour the electric as the best solution, although opponents point out that lowered pollution in cities is won only at the expense of greater pollution from power stations. However, as these turn from coal to gas or nuclear power that problem should be less of a threat. The most pressing needs are for a battery giving still greater range, and larger-scale production so that the cost of an electric can be reduced to a figure competitive with that of a petrol or diesel vehicle.

FURTHER READING

Few books are devoted specifically to battery-electric vehicles, but some that are are included in this list:

De Boer, Roger F. *Birmingham's Electric Dustcarts*. Birmingham & Midland Motor Omnibus Trust, 1990.
Hills, S.M. *Battery Electric Vehicles*. Newnes, 1943.
Jeudy, Jean-Gabriel. *Camions de France*. Massin, 1994. Sovel, Stela and other French vehicles are comprehensively covered.
Kaye, David. *British Battery Electric Buses*. Oakwood Press, 1976.

Kennedy, Rankin. *The Book of the Motor Car*. Caxton, 1913. Technical coverage of early vehicles.
Shacket, Sheldon R. *The Complete Book of Electric Vehicles*. Millington Books, 1980.
Wakefield, Ernest H. *History of the Electric Automobile*. Society of Automotive Engineers, Warrendale, Pa, 1994.

PLACES TO VISIT

Museum displays may be altered, and readers are advised to telephone before visiting in order to avoid disappointment.

Birmingham and Midland Museum of Transport, Chapel Lane, Wythall, Birmingham B47 6JX. Telephone: 01564 826471. Forty battery-electric vehicles, mostly milk floats, of which twenty-two are on display.
Birmingham Museum of Science and Industry, Newhall Street, Birmingham B3 1RZ. Telephone: 0121-235 1661. 1938 Electricars DV4 refuse collector.
British Commercial Vehicle Museum, King Street, Leyland, Preston, Lancashire PR5 1LE. Telephone: 01772 451011. 1980 Bedford CF Lucas van.
East Anglia Transport Museum, Chapel Road, Carlton Colville, Lowestoft, Suffolk NR33 8BL. Telephone: 01502 569399. 1922 Ransomes Orwell tower wagon.
Heritage Motor Centre, Banbury Road, Gaydon, Warwick CV35 0BJ. Telephone: 01926 641188. 1972 Leyland Crompton Electricar saloon, 1977 Lucas taxi (in store).
Ipswich Transport Museum, Old Trolleybus Depot, Cobham Road, Ipswich, Suffolk IP3 9JD. Telephone: 01473 715666. 1914 and 1915 Ransomes lorries, 1948 Smiths-NCB milk float, 1951 Morrison-Electricar coal lorry, two 1967 Enfield saloons, 1984 Brush Pony van, 1983 Leyland Sherpa conversion, 1980s Pandora bicycle.
Museum of British Road Transport, St Agnes Lane, Hales Street, Coventry, West Midlands CV1 1PN. Telephone: 01203 832425. 1956 Midland milk float, 1979 Lanchester Polytechnic car, 1985 UDAP (Coventry University) car, 1985 Sinclair C5 (two), 1987 City Wheels car.
Museum of Transport – Greater Manchester, Boyle Street, Cheetham, Manchester M8 8UW. Telephone: 0161-205 1082 or 2122. 1974 Seddon-Chloride fifty-seater bus, 1975 Seddon-Lucas twenty-seven seater bus.
National Motor Museum, John Montagu Building, Beaulieu, Brockenhurst, Hampshire SO42 7ZN. Telephone: 01590 612345. 1897 Bersey cab, 1947 Brush Pony milk float, 1901 Columbia stanhope, 1939 Harrods van.
Science Museum, Exhibition Road, South Kensington, London SW7 2DD. Telephone: 0171-938 8000. 1967 Daf 44 converted to battery propulsion.
Science Museum Store, Red Barn Gate, Wroughton Airfield, Swindon, Wiltshire SN4 9NS. Telephone: 01793 814466. 1939 Harrods van, 1967 Ford Comuta (in store).
Snibston Discovery Park, Ashby Road, Coalville, Leicestershire LE6 2LN. Telephone: 01530 510851. 1927 Electricars dustcart (in store), 1935 Wilson ice-cream van, 1957 Harbilt milk float, 1967 Morris Traveller conversion.
Southern Electric Museum, The Old Power Station, Bargates, Christchurch, Dorset BH23 1QE. Telephone: 01202 480467. 1976 Enfield saloon, 1980 Dodge tower wagon.
Streetlife – Hull Museum of Transport, 36 High Street, Hull, North Humberside. Telephone: 01482 593902. 1900 Cleveland stanhope.

CLUB

The Battery Vehicle Society: Secretary, Richard Pryor, 3 Blandford St Mary, Blandford Forum, Dorset DT11 9LH. The most important organisation for battery vehicles, it publishes a quarterly journal, *Battery Vehicle Review*, in which details of forthcoming battery-vehicle gatherings are listed.